The Thousandaire Challenge

your blueprints to financial stability

by

Adam Rivon

Bloomington, IN Milton Keynes, UK

 authorHOUSE®

AuthorHouse™
1663 Liberty Drive, Suite 200
Bloomington, IN 47403
www.authorhouse.com
Phone: 1-800-839-8640

AuthorHouse™ UK Ltd.
500 Avebury Boulevard
Central Milton Keynes, MK9 2BE
www.authorhouse.co.uk
Phone: 08001974150

First published by AuthorHouse 3/1/2007

ISBN: 978-1-4259-8394-9 (sc)

Printed in the United States of America
Bloomington, Indiana

This book is printed on acid-free paper.

Table of Contents

Acknowledgements

It is my determined purpose to know God and the power of his resurrection; to love, lead, and inspire others to live a good life…constant and never-ending improvement. Gracious thanks goes to the woman of my dreams, Misty, my best friend, wife, and lover. Thank you to my loving family for your encouraging words and support. I also want to give a special thanks to my spiritual father Bishop T. D. Jakes for the inspiration to write and other leaders that have guided me to include Joyce Myer, Creflo Dollar, Tony Robins, and all the personal mentors who've helped direct my life of purpose.

Foreward

The Purpose of this book:
What's in it for you?

The American Dream is the faith held by many in the United States of America that through hard work, courage, and determination one can achieve financial prosperity, a better, richer, and fuller life; as James Truslow Adams wrote in the *Epic of America*, 1931.

Today, 96% of America will retire dependant on the government. How's your dream evolving? When is the last time you thought about your retirement plan or spoke to an advisor? If you haven't, what's the reason? Why do we spend more time planning our vacations than we do our finances? Why do you work everyday? Are you planning to work until the day you die? It's looking that way if you don't get a plan, and statistics show that 80% of Americans don't even enjoy their work environment. So, do you subsequently plan to be unhappy the remainder of your life? Something has to be done, because the majority of us spend more than we make. So, how do we change? The truth is that it's all in your mind, you've been enslaved. We see what master has and we want it; with out going though the same process of attaining it. Who then is you master? Most likely, your master is the debt that you hold, a person you envy, or maybe it's the Hollywood lifestyle. Look at it this way, if you owe money to anyone and you want to pay them back then you are bonded, or in bondage until you repay them. So you work it off at a place that most likely you don't enjoy. Eventually, you began to owe more than you make and a fear of job loss develops, because how would you make your mortgage payment, child's catholic school tuition or car note with out a job. You're determined to change, so you're saving money or making payments to the bank or credit cards but there's little to nothing available at months end and your child or spouse request that thing, that thing that they've longed for days, and you give in. The cycle has begun. This book is dedicated to keeping you out of the cycle of debt, and assisting you in becoming a THOUSANDAIRE. What is this you thousandaire you ask. It will be revealed as we progress.

Some of you may be saying HELP I AM ALREADY IN DEBT!

If you've picked up this book for the soul purpose of getting out of debt **quickly**, I may not be able to help you. People always ask, should they take up a consolidation loan. The answer is maybe, but only if you have to. It is my hope that you will be able to answer that question for yourself once you've completed this book. If you do decide to make such a move, promise yourself, that you will hold fast to the precepts of this book. Otherwise, you will end up in the same predicament two years from now. Life isn't always easy and to date maybe you haven't been very successful in managing your finances, but I hope to help you change that by giving you the knowledge and understanding of what to do.

Discipline-training expected to produce a specific character or pattern of belief. In your case discipline will produce financial well being and stability. You will need to train yourself in order to change your situation. You've handled money your way, your entire life, but I will propose to you some simple changes in the ways you approach, use and think about money. Hopefully, if you pay close attention to what's written, use the examples, fill them in with your personnel information, and truly seek to improve, you will see drastic changes take place in your finances and in your life. Because, when you show commitment in your finances, you also show a commitment to yourself and those whom are closest to you. If you strive to become a thousandaire, and work consistently and never cease to improve, your life will never again be the same. Gone are the days of confusion and lack. Stay tuned, because I will be introducing new terms and teaching you what it takes to become a thousandaire.

There are a few assumptions I make in this writing this book: 1. You want to improve your current situation 2. You're ready to change some bad habits 3. You're willing to commit to life improvement. If you're unwilling to commit to all three covenants, this book will not help you improve your lifestyle.

If you are ready to commit to change and enter into a new dimension of peace and prosperity then let's proceed.

Prioritizing Life

Wisdom is supreme; therefore get wisdom. Though
it cost all you have, get understanding
Proverbs 4:7 NIV bible

What's most important in your life? To some, it's family, and for others, it may be money, cars, women, and happiness. Your finances are ordered in accordance with how you've ordered your life. Chaotic finances will most likely show up in a chaotic lifestyle.

Much research has been conducted on the subject of need versus wants, and it is worth reviewing what has been found to be our basic human needs. This can help you re-center and focus to ensure that your needs are being met.

Renowned psychologist Abraham Maslow created the basic needs pyramid in 1953. Let's review his research and see how it applies to your life:

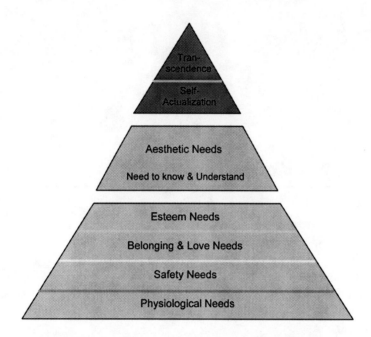

Understand that each need is built on another, so if you are deficient in one, you can still move to greater heights, but your life will be unstable. The lower section makes-up your deficiency needs. You will always attempt to correct this deficiency/void need, first, when a problem arises. This is when you don't know why you do a certain thing, but you know that it is some how connected to your childhood years.

<u>Physiological</u>: These are the most basic needs to function well in society: self worth, shelter, and food. They also correlate directly to your finances, in that you should always prioritize yourself, your housing, and your subsistence. In other words, don't buy new rims for your car with the rent money.

<u>Safety</u>: This is being able to protect those you love. How safe is your neighborhood and how does it effect the inhabitants? Where do you keep your money? Do you have insurance? The safest places are generally the most prosperous places. Everyone wants a safe environment for his or her children, right?

<u>Love</u>: This is being accepted and having affiliations. If your love cup is full, then there's no reason to spend all your money at the clubs or bars.

<u>Esteem</u>: This is being able to achieve, being competent, and gaining approval and recognition. Financially, you will achieve small goals that will bring you confidence and pride on your way to becoming a thousandaire.

All of these together make up the deficiency needs, and the next levels are the growth needs. Maslow believed that individuals will never act on the growth needs until deficiency needs are met. This is why there are young people who make you say, "I just know he/she is going to make something of him or herself," but they never do. This is why many families of today are in debt up to their eyeballs. This is why we're still trying to keep up with the Joneses. Do you have a Jones (master) that you've been trying emulate, but with little or no guidance? Just because Bob, who lives in your neighborhood and makes a similar salary, got a new car and living room set, doesn't mean that you are able to have or deserve the same thing, right now. You don't know what Bob may have gone with out, or has done in order to get what he received. You don't have to accept what society hands to you as being for you, right now. In order to be successful in managing our finances, we have to be able to distinguish between our lives' needs and wants. Then you must have the discipline to only purchase as you've planned, and not as you feel. There is so much more in this principle that I would like to share, but I will save it for another forum, because it ties into other societal issues.

Taking it to the Next Level

The next need in your finances is growth, and is subdivided into four levels. Individuals in this season of life are characterized by some level of financial security and direction. They've mastered their basic needs, seek to understand more, and explore more in various financial instruments. They have established order and control over their money. These individuals could lose their jobs today and would not sweat. These people are good candidates for and may have already attained thousandaire status. We'll discuss more on this term later, but know for now that it is your next destination.

Maslow differentiated the growth need of self-actualization, specifically naming two lower-level growth needs prior to the general level of self-actualization, which are cognitive and aesthetic (Maslow and Lowery, 1998) and one need beyond actualization, which is transcendence. Self-actualized people are characterized by the following:

being problem-focused, incorporating an ongoing freshness or appreciation for life a concern about personal growth, and the ability to have peak experiences (Maslow, 1971). They are:

1) <u>Cognitive</u>: to know, to understand, and explore--here, you've become a hunter-gatherer, constantly seeking and attaining

improvement, investments, and information that will give you an edge or step up in your finances;

2) <u>Aesthetic</u>: symmetry, order, and beauty--this phase of your financial life is when you've gathered and improved, and now seek stability and sanctity; It is my goal to get you to this level of understanding and financial well being.

3) <u>Self-actualization</u>: to find self-fulfillment and realize one's true potential and purpose--you begin not only to understand your purpose, but actually walk in it;

4) <u>Transcendence</u>: to connect to something beyond the ego or material world--here you help others find self-fulfillment and realize their potential.

Maslow's basic position is that as one becomes more self-actualized and transcends, he/she has developed wisdom that allows him/her to automatically know how to plan and react in a wide variety of situations. It is here that we all hope to be because it is here that we attain the fulfillment of our life's purpose.

The THOUSANDAIRE is more than just a net worth. It's a mindset. It's understanding your financial position and knowing when to explore new options. It's developing stability through organized and deliberate financial statements. Ultimately, you will find your purpose and guide your finances and life in that direction. When you understand why you were placed on this Earth and figure out what legacy you would like to leave, as a thousandaire, you will have already ordered your finances to move in that direction, at any moment. The thousandaires of today are the millionaires of tomorrow!

Climbing Mountains

True ballers transcend. This is Maslow's highest principal and characterizes our ultimate financial position. Oprah Winfrey and Bill Gates epitomize this principle, but you may also know of individuals that operate in this realm who are not famous. These people have taken all the previous financial steps and operate totally in their God-given gifts. They not only reach out to others, but they pull them up, by going above and beyond. They are philanthropic, but they don't have to be billionaires or famous. They understand who they are and are happy with their positions in life. They've tapped into the ultimate source of life and spirit: their purpose. They spend 95 percent of their time dealing with purpose and 5 percent with non-purpose-driven issues. So, think about what percentage of your time and money goes to non-purpose-driven items or events.

TAKE HOME

We have to take care of our basic financial needs before we can ever achieve financial stability. You have to distinguish between needs and wants in order to establish controls over your money. Finally, choose to take it to the next level, and ultimately plan to operate efficiently in your life's purpose, and that's what you'll do best, whether scrubbing floors or wearing scrubs.

Lead Me to the Water

*The reason most people never reach their goals is that
they don't define them, or ever seriously consider them
as believable or achievable. Winners can tell you where
they are going, what they plan to do along the way,
and who will be sharing the adventure with them.*

Denis Watley

Now, you understand needs versus wants, but will still need direction and motivation in order to stay the course. Too many people are giving up on their dreams because of life's setbacks (premature pregnancy, debt, deaths, or shifts in our family structures). It is time to re-focus and establish a vision for your family. Without a vision, we will always fail in our finances. Maybe you've attempted and were unsuccessful several times. Maybe this isn't the first book on finances that you've read, and the others didn't help. Here is a clue: you're going to have to deal with your psyche in order to improve your situation.

If you continue to do what you've always done, you will continue to get what you have always gotten. Most likely, it is not the number of attempts, but the approach that has brought you to no resolution. Now may not be the time to get back on the track, but eventually you will. Also, know that the road of success can be very long and generally ninety-eight of one hundred exits lead to failure. King of comedy, Steve Harvey reminds us that it is never too late to have a success story. So stay the course, and if you've already exited too soon, you can always get back on the highway.

Here's another nugget: one can never transcend without success in one's personal ventures and finances. Success is also very pervasive because it is wrapped up in the journey; therefore, you could arrive and not know. This is why you'll need to set some goals or benchmarks that help you keep track along the way. You set your own parameter for success, and so, it must *not* be constantly moving, otherwise you will never arrive.

Seriously, take an hour or more to considered these topics, now! I recommend that you write down some goals and review them with a significant other. This will serve as both a sobriety test and an accountability measure, because you're only accountable to what you confess. You should develop a set of both long-term and short-term goals. Write them down first, and then put them away until we require them later.

Here are some tips to assist you: Be smart in goal-setting.

Specific: Goals must be specific. To say "I want more money by the end of the year" is meaningless. How much more money? Which year are you referring to?

Example: I expect to save $1,000 this year for my retirement!

Measurable: How will you know when you've achieved it? This relates back to how specific you've been initially. Use numbers, quantities, or capacities you can track by how much you exceeded your goal or have fallen short.

Example: I will sell fifty-five houses and settle on fifty of them, this year!

Action-oriented: This is incredibly important. The world rewards action. So begin to take action towards it. For example, if you want more money, you may look at cutting out unnecessary expenditures.

Example: I will save $100 per month by only eating out four times a month!

Realistic: If you want to be a millionaire by the end of the year, but the money in your bank account only shows double-digit integers, short of winning the lottery, you're unlikely to achieve this. If so, look at increasing the amount of time you give yourself to achieve this goal.

Example: I will become a millionaire in ten years with the patent for my cure for the common cold!

Time-based: When do you hope to achieve this goal: one month, three months, six months, a year, or five years? Be specific and hold yourself to the fire.

The key to setting goals is to set the bar high and think big, then allowing enough time to do things incrementally.

Write down your goals (or draw or paint them, etc.). It helps to make them real where you can see them, rather than letting them swirl about endlessly in your head, where they have no outlet. This will also help to keep you on track. Take pictures that inspire you toward them and place them in places you visit frequently, like your work desk, home refrigerator, office computer, bathroom vanity, or even where you do your business--the toilet. Just don't flush them.

Also, unless someone is critical to helping you achieve your goal(s), do not freely share them with others. The negative attitude from friends, family, and neighbors can drag you down quickly, but the accolades of one significant other can propel you to success quicker. So be very cautious and guard your personal goals, because most people will not openly applaud your success ventures.

I recommend writing one- and five-year goals for your finances, but if you haven't done the same for you life and career, you should do them in correlation with these. You should also link a minimum of three financial goals to your one- and five-year life goals.

Okay, go ahead, do it now, and pick it back up in an hour or later.

Write the vision, and make it plain upon
tables, that he may run that readeth it.

Habakkuk 2: 2

Okay, do so now.

Short-term (this year/month):

_____

_____

_____

_____

Long-term (next year/five years):

_____

_____

_____

_____

What is your vision for your life? Where do you want to be spiritually, financially, and physically in one, five, and ten years from now? Give your money a purpose that it may be fruitful; without purpose, it will wither from your pockets.

All subsequent chapters will include the Why/Action section, our common sense check, and the Spoken Word sections, our confession, which must be spoken aloud.

WHY:

So, why write down your goals? Write them down because on a daily basis, you can be inundated with information and tasks, but this sheet of purpose will keep you mindful of what is most important in your life!

SPOKEN WORD:➤➤➤

I have written these goals on paper and I will use them to fulfill my life's purpose.

The Foundation

Okay, now that you have the goals, let's break them down into tasks.

Example #1: Save $10,000 for my emergency fund by the end of this year!

    a.   (how) I need to set up an automatic allotment from my checking that goes to savings in the amount of $830 per month.

    b.   (reality) After laying out my budget for the year, I will only have $600 of expendable cash at the end of each month.

    c.   (adjustment) I can reasonably expect to save $500 per month, because I will need a buffer for unexpected expenses of $100 each month. This would only be $6,000 for the year in my emergency nest egg. If I truly desire to save the extra $4k, then maybe I can find a side job, or cut back in some other areas.

Example #1 (revised): I will save $6,000 for my emergency fund by this years end.

Recommendation:

Because this is an emergency fund, in this situation, it may be best to defer some of your major purchases in order to reach this goal as soon as possible. After you attain any of your goals, you should treat yourself to some small reward, in recognition of your accomplishment. This could be as simple as a movie night with someone special. The key is to mark the milestone for your own remembrance.

Example #2: Reduce my credit card debt to $5,000, and reduce the number of cards that I have down to 2.

a. (how) Cut all the non-essential cards (i.e. department stores, jewelry stores, etc.), and consolidate payments.
b. (reality) You're apprehensive about cutting ten cards because they give you some euphoric sense of luxury. Also, after looking over your available cash and credit limits, you only have $200 available to pay down debt.
c. (adjust) You can reasonably consolidate all but three of your cards, with a total debt of $9,800. With the extra $200 available to pay down debt, you realize that you will probably get down to about $6,500 by December of this year.

Example #2 (revised): I will reduce my credit card debt to $5,000 in the next 18 months and reduce the number of credit cards I hold to 3 by this year's end in order to create more financial stability.

Recommendation:

Cut the cards, because it is apparent that you're out of control, so it is of the utmost importance to remove the temptation and go to an all-cash system, for a season. Also, you may notice that there are a few luxuries that, if curtailed, could save you an additional $150 per month, and could shorten your time horizon or act as a buffer for the interim.

Although, in the examples above, you have some reduction-spending recommendations, recognize that the intent is not to limit your ability to enjoy your money, but to develop a stable and safe foundation. You will eventually reap even more fun and less stress, because you learn to live within and below your means. Realize also that the average millionaire in America drives a five- to ten-year-old vehicle, saves more than he or she spends, and is focused in all his or her endeavors. That is a far cry from what Hollywood has sold to you as the life.

Sam Walton, once the world's wealthiest man, drove a beat-up old Ford, and he was never seen wearing a Louis Vuitton anything. These are his legacy's ten commandments:

1. Commit to your goals
2. Share your rewards
3. Energize your colleagues
4. Communicate all you know!
5. Value your associates
6. Celebrate your success
7. Listen to everyone
8. Deliver more than you promise
9. Work smarter than others
10. Blaze your own path!

Now, this was Sam's chosen lifestyle, and I am not advocating a life with no luxuries, but I do ask that you think before you buy. For more, read Sam Walton, Made in America, Little Rock. Bantam, 1993.

It is about focus, because what you focus on or magnify becomes larger. Let's say it has always been your goal to be a pharmacy technician, but after graduating high school, things didn't turn out so well. You attempted school, but ran out of money, so you had to get a job and skip a semester. It turned into two, and you started making decent money. So, you began to spend more money and save less. After being out of school for a year, you've now lost some confidence in your ability to finish. Friends in jest may have even said some things, and now three years have passed. You realize that the extra money hasn't made you happy, but life has begun to put you in a vice. Your original goal was to save money for school, but now you have more bills than you started with and less available cash. You feel victimized, but it was a series of bad choices and a lack of focus that have directed your fate.

Now, this story is fiction, but many of you can relate to the story. So, how do you get back on the right course? Well, it starts by doing what you've hopefully already begun. Re-center by setting some goals and having a vision of where you're going, and how you'd like your life to turn out. Without a vision, an outlook for success, you have no reason to improve on a daily basis. You lose your ability to succeed, because you have nothing to achieve. Your life becomes predicated on your circumstances and feelings. Your emotions control your finances, and your pocketbook develops holes.

Today, you need to take some form of action on every goal that you've written. If it was a life goal to lose weight, you must take action, now. Get up now and join the gym, or if your goal was to save more money, then open a savings account, today. Get up and drive to the bank now.

Share your vision with me online at www.adamrivon.com. I would love to see your progress and encourage you along the way.

The Facts

You land a new job and you're so happy that you decide to celebrate. You and some friends go out for fun and drinks. Now, you haven't actually been paid yet, but you're expecting an increase in pay of $200 per month. You figure, for your success, you can now afford to buy some extra things that you've been holding out for. Without a thought about the facts, your increase in pay can quickly become an even larger increase in debt. It's called consumer confidence, and marketing companies feed on this. Essentially, it is consumers' appraisal of current conditions and their expectations for the future. Expectations make up 60 percent of the total index, with current conditions accounting for the other 40 percent.

In other words, how do you feel about spending your money? So you can see how marketing companies could use this index to eat away all your increase. Commercials say you work hard, so you deserve to reward yourself with a really expensive diamond or a weekend at the casino. Then you take the bait and make the trip, without an observance of the facts. You landed the new job, and suddenly the car problems escalate to a breakdown, so you purchase the latest and greatest thing. Had you followed the maintenance schedule and allocated the proper amount of funds, you could have avoided a major breakdown; now you've added hundreds to the car note and insurance in addition to the new maintenance schedule and cost. But it might be likely that you will not follow this schedule for the new vehicle, because you've increased your payments and have begun spending above that of your pay raise, and you haven't, yet, received your first check! Without consulting the facts you will continually fall into the same debt cycle for life. So what are these facts that I continue referring to? They are your current financial picture. How then do we retrieve this picture? It is hidden inside your financial documents: a budget or cash flow statement. Do you have the available cash flow to make a major purchase (X), today? Is your credit rating high enough to get the best interest rate or even the one you need, based on your available cash? Does this purchase fit into your bigger picture, the annual budget, or your vision?

On that note, do you have an outline or idea of the things that you want to purchase or complete this year? Know that without it, you are traveling down a path with no end, wearing a blindfold. So, you're always reacting to events and adjusting based on how you feel, as opposed to the facts, your current financial position. In the upcoming chapters, you will learn how to set up a tracking system for your finances. You will learn everything from the basics of balancing a checkbook or card to balancing your annual budget. This will assist you in making decisions for the greater good of your family and keep you off the creditor's deadbeat radar.

Assessing Your Current State

If money is your hope for independence you will never have it. The only real security that a man will have in this world is a reserve of knowledge, experience, and ability.

Henry Ford

Up until now you may have been living from check to check, but after the next few chapters, you will have the knowledge base to set up a monthly budget and eventually work from an annual system. There are several bad reasons that you live hand-to-mouth, and most likely the amount you earn has little to do with this. If you're like most, it's a lack of spending discipline; others fear financial planning; so many more are just taught bad habits from their parents. Whether these descriptions fit you or yours is a different issue; we're going to erase the past and leap into our future with a renewed sense of control over our resources.

The average American spends more time planning a vacation than his or her retirement. Once, my brother asked, "How much of your monthly spending is unaccounted for?" In confusion, I stated, "None," and he was totally shocked at this revelation. Why, you may ask? It was because the majority of his income was spent each month on a whim. The only thing he knew was that his bills were paid. At the end of each bill cycle, the amount of money remaining determined the amount of fun he experienced on the weekend or at the club. Now, I am by no means opposed to having fun or having drinks, but why not set some limits? This way, at the end of each month, you have a little extra for emergencies and other conveniences.

Personal Finance 101

I define personal finance as the process of earning, managing/ allocating, controlling, and then dispensing your money. This section is a little tricky, so make sure that you are alert before you begin.

Let's get started. First, you have to understand how to balance your books. For me, pictures work best, so I'll attempt to use as many diagrams as possible. We will start with your balance sheet and bank statement, and then move to an income/cash flow statement, but first here are some accounting basics.

ASSETS=LIABILITIES + OWNER'S EQUITY
(A=L+E)

* ❖ Assets are money, vehicles, homes, stocks, bonds, and cash owed to you.
  * ▪ This is the stuff in your possession, whether partially or fully owned.
* ❖ Liabilities are loans, notes, taxes, and mortgages.
  * ▪ This is the stuff you owe.
* ❖ Owner's equity
  * ➢ This is your net worth.
  * ➢ This is the value/percentage of the stuff you actually own.
* • Subsequently, A-L=E and A-E=L.

- Both sides of the equation must be equal in order for it to be in balance.

EXAMPLE:

A- You have a car worth $22,000.

B- You pay a note, with a current balance of $11,200.

C- If you sold the car, at its full value today, you would keep $10,800.

(a) 22,000 = (L) 11,200 + (E) 10,800

This is simple enough, and you may now see how everything that you possess can be categorized by this system. Very smart accountants developed a way to record transactions in a balance sheet. That is a statement or picture of your assets and liabilities on a specific date. They decided to use duel entry system of debits (DR) and credits (CR), and have regulated that you must have a DR and a corresponding CR in order to record a transaction. Here is how it works:

Assets are (+) increased with a DR and (-) decreased with a CR.
Liabilities and owner's equity are (+) increased with a CR and (-) decreased with a DR.
Example: you purchase a new computer for $1,500 cash

ASSETS	LIABILITIES	OWNER'S EQUITY
DR	-	CR
+$1500 computer	0	+$1500 owned

- Let's say you financed the deal 100 percent.

ASSETS	LIABILITIES	OWNER'S EQUITY
DR	CR	-
+$1500 computer	+$1500 loaned	0

- This time, you financed 50 percent.

ASSETS	LIABILITIES	OWNER'S EQUITY
DR	CR	CR
+$1500 computer	+$750 loaned	+$750 owned

- Finally, you sold the computer for the same price you purchased it.

ASSETS	LIABILITIES	OWNER'S EQUITY
CR and DR	-	-
-$1500 computer and +$1500 cash	0	0

Now, you are either lost or wondering why I took you through these scenarios. So now, I'll help you discern how these transactions relate to your bank statement. Okay, when you put money in the bank, the bank then owes you money. When you deposit $100 into your savings, the bank records the transaction in their books like this:

ASSETS	LIABILITIES	OWNER'S EQUITY
DR	CR	-
$100	$100	0
the bank has	The bank owes you	

Side note: so how does the bank make money? Historically, it makes money by charging fees and lending your savings out to others for a profit. Because consumers are savvy, the trend has moved banking away from charging you fees and now the industry primarily makes money through loans and other services offered.

Have you ever wondered why, when you deposit money, your account is credited (CR) and when you spend money, your account is debited (DR)? Now you know why banks give you a debit card, which, when used, will decrease their liability to you.

- You spent $100 on a purchase with your debit card. The bank records:

ASSETS	LIABILITIES	OWNER'S EQUITY
CR	DR	-
-$100	-$100	0

Now that you have a foundation on the terminology, let's balance the books and set up a balance sheet. First, you have to understand the importance of each, but if you've ever had a check bounce, then you already know. It's humiliating. This is the first step to freedom. Know where you stand today, so you can properly plan where you want to be tomorrow. The following is an example month's transactions:

1. Electric bill: $200
2. Rent: $900
3. Heating gas: $30
4. Phone: $120
5. Cable: $50
6. Car note: $533
7. Paycheck: $2,593.68
8. Student Loan: $245
9. Internet: $25.68

We'll use these events and document them in our checkbook that has a starting balance of $1,500.

Description	DR	CR	BAL
Your check book log and the account number would be here.			
Starting balance			1,500
Electric bill	200		1,300
Rent	900		400
Gas	30		370
Phone	120		250
Cable	50		200
Car note	533		-333
Paycheck		2,593.68	2,260.68
Student loan	245		2,015.68
Internet	25.68		1,900
ENDING BAL			1,900

- Here is a second sheet for you to fill in with your transactions this week:
- This is similar to the transaction log you would find in a checkbook

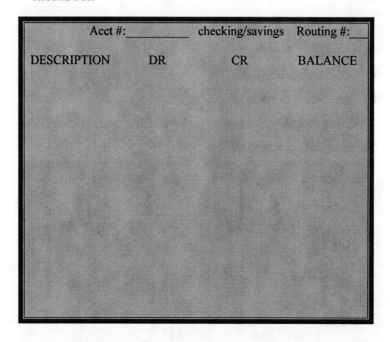

Can you, now, understand why you're required to keep track of each transaction? If you have more activity in your checking account, it is okay for our purposes, now, just to do a partial log. Also, learn to be accurate with your records, so that you don't have to go back later to find simple mistakes, and always keep tabs on your balance. If you've never balanced your books, you will need to set a point at which to start. A good rule of thumb is to go back to the beginning of the current fiscal or operating period, or to your fist paycheck of the previous month.

Analysis:

Through our example, we can see the importance of tracking, because had we done so, as the days progressed, we could have delayed paying the cable and car note until after we got paid. This would have prevented what will most likely be an additional bank charge. With proper planning, most creditors are flexible, and had we requested to change a few payment dates or verified that the payments had to be processed on that date, we would have avoided the overdraft on our account. This is very important, because if we ever wanted to borrow money from our banking institution, we are less likely to receive a loan if we have a history of insufficient funds.

Here marks the day you began making better decisions. You are informed. Finally, experience tracking transactions allows you to balance the books quicker and more efficiently. Since you have all the transactions listed in your booklet, the only other thing to do is subtract from your balance any additional listed charges to your account found on the bank's statement. When you receive the monthly statement, you are also likely to see a $25 charge for overdraft/ insufficient funds and any ATM fees or secondary charges. This is where the balancing begins. Now we must compare records. Sometimes banks will separate deposits from checks from debit card transactions. Don't be confused--you should just use your transaction log as a guide. I suggest using a red pen and placing a dot next to your recorded transactions and the bank's as you match them and move down the statement in comparison. Use your book as the standard and follow it chronologically. This way, you know whether all of your transactions have been recorded by the bank. Once you get to the bottom, you will probably have a few checks or transactions that haven't cleared the bank, and so you leave them blank.

a. If transactions haven't cleared the bank, they are generally termed outstanding (i.e. outstanding checks/deposits).

b. Then, as you glance at the bank statement, there may be other bank charges that you don't have listed, because you didn't know what the exact amounts were. You should subtract these charges from your log book.

c. Then subtract any outstanding checks from the bank's statement (DR), because they're on your log, but not in their records.

d. Finally, deposits from your log that are not on the statement should be added to the bank's statement (CR).

Assuming you have recorded all of your transactions correctly, congratulations--you are balanced. If any small discrepancies are present, check your math! If you're still not balancing, go back through each transaction, line by line, until you note a discrepancy in one of the account records. If the problem is on your side, correct it, and if it's on the bank's side, you will need to call and be sure to communicate this fact to them.

Once my bank erroneously deposited $17,532.89, and then in a correction, subtracted $20,876.11. This caused an overdraft of $25, but because I had online banking, I was able to catch this error the same day. I called and explained my position, and they of course quickly corrected the situation.

TAKE AWAY

In this chapter, we've learned the basics and see that it takes planning and consistency to manage your books properly, but after working this process for a few months, it will become second nature. The benefits are endless, and as time goes by, you will develop greater and easier methods of tracking.

1. How do you know if you need a loan, if you don't know how much money you have?
2. Would you give money to a person that didn't know what he or she had or needed, or when he or she could repay you?
3. How much interest would you charge a person that never has enough money to pay his or her own bills?
4. Is it better to know who you can't pay this month and call them with a plan or just wait for the repossession man to show up?

ACTION:

Gather all your bills from last month, along with your bank statements, and last year's W-2 prior to reading the next chapter.

SPOKEN WORD ➤➤➤

All my financial books are regularly balanced, and I consider the facts before making any purchases.

Living for the Day?

It's Friday night, and you've heeded the sound personal financial guidance. You've been tracking transactions and you know that you have $100 in the bank. Some friends ask you to have a night on the town, and you think it is about time you were rewarded for your efforts, so you stop by an ATM. Then, you and the gang hit the road for downtown (X). The clubs have a $20 entry fee on the weekend. The music is loud, the crowd is wild, and you decide to treat everyone to their first round of drinks. There are five of you together, and you end up over the course of the night paying for another round. The average cost of drinks that night came to just over $7. You end up paying $80 for your tab. You have a wonderful time at the party, meeting people dancing and reminiscing, so you decide to grab a bite to eat to chill your buzz. The bill comes in around $10; you reach into your pocket and realize that you're out of cash, so you use the credit card instead. You were paid on Friday, so you figure you'll have extra cash on Monday. This type of harmless overspending is where the cycle begins. Monday comes, and you forget that it was also the end of your billing cycle, so cash is actually reduced again. You decide to use credit as a buffer until the cash increases, and your debt slowly inches upward and over $1,000. You are motivated to pay the card off and diligently attempted to do so, but something always seemed to pop up.

Know that things will continue to pop up as long as you live. It is proper planning that acts as a buffer to prevent you from massive fluctuations in lifestyle. Stuff will always happen, but you're much better prepared if you live for the day and plan for tomorrow.

What now? You've developed $9-13K in credit card debt over the last few years, and there seems to be no letting up. Interest rates are through the roof, and if you pay attention to the credit cards' small print, it says that by paying the minimum payment for (X) amount of debt, it will take you seven years to pay-off, assuming you never use the card again. You will have paid three or four times what was actually spent. Ladies by the time you pay this card off, that suit you bought for $50 on a 50 percent clearance sale will actually cost you $150-200. I'm glad you got it on sale; otherwise, you would have paid $300-400 for the same suit. Is it worth it? Did the suit even last as long as your payment?

Sales are what get most shoppers, but let us revert to Maslow. We must know our needs versus wants, and only make purchases that are planned. It sounds simple enough, but it takes discipline to follow though.

In this section, we will focus on remodeling your finances through budgeting.

Okay, don't put the book down so fast; I've kept you interested so far, and I will attempt to make this section fun as well. "But you didn't say anything about budgeting." Sure I did; since the beginning, I have emphasized the need for planning. These two words are synonymous.

The purpose of a budget is to plan your financial decisions for each month and year. It's also important to have goals and a vision, because without them, there are no benchmarks for your budget, E.g. goals for Mr. Jones 2006:

1. Learn to play the piano
2. Become debt-free

Remember, goals should be SMART. What makes you happy? Simple things, even the things you do on a daily basis, should be integrated into your budget. Its purpose is to review and prioritize monetary events in your life for a specific period of time. This is generally in one month or year increments.

Second, it allows you to see a bigger picture, or a bird's eye view, if you will. If I ask you how much money you make or what your salary is, you could probably tell me in hourly or annual terms pretty quickly and succinctly, but how much do you keep? Most likely, you don't know. Now, you're probably looking for a check stub, but at this point, the actual number isn't as important as the thought process. You have to understand that it's not what you make that is important. You get a raise or a new job and for argument, let's say your salary will be $30,000 per year. You've recently graduated from college and you're ecstatic. Your first check arrives, and you run to your favorite store to purchase that dress, those shoes, or that thing that you been dying to have. Once you arrive home from shopping, you pick up the mail and it's full of bills. You've got rent ($900), electric ($200), gas ($30), phone ($120), and cable ($50) bills waiting for you, totaling $1,300. You quickly add them up and realize that you didn't make enough to pay for your clothes and the bills. So what do you do?

You set up a budget to keep track of what you will have going on. What should it include?

First, it should include your gross and net income: how much you make before and after taxes. This is important because you should know what the government is taking, and you cannot budget for something that you don't have.

Second, subtract any employer deductions. These should include, but are not limited to, 401k plan, and health and life insurance deductions. These are also important, because as time goes on, you may need to adjust them, based on your needs; because they are generally a fixed cost, you will not need to adjust them often.

Now after pulling out all of this information, we can see that you actually bring home $25,500 after taxes and $22,856 after deductions. This comes to $1,904.67 per month and not $2,500.00. We will use these numbers for the basic formulation of our budget model.

MODEL:

Alright, we know what you make. Now let's look into what you spend, so that we may derive what you are able to keep! The truth is that there isn't always money to keep. We'll review that later, but for now, I will assume you do have available cash at the end of the month. Take your actual bills into consideration. Here are the purchases we listed earlier:

Liabilities: Accounts Payable		
Description	DR(+)	CR(-)
Electric bill		200.00
Rent		900.00
Gas		30.00
Phone		120.00
Cable		50.00
Car note		533.00
Student loan		.00
Internet		25.68

Your income is $1904.67.

We compute and see there is only $45.99 remaining that will allow you to feed and groom yourself, give to charity, and socialize. Obviously, this is not going to work. So, what do you do next? You must prioritize, by understanding needs versus wants. Some of us are living with this type of budget and have never realized it, because we didn't know how much we made nor brought home, and have never rolled all of the bills up into a summary statement. We all need a place to stay, but make sure that you aren't living above your means. Most mortgage companies follow a one-third rule, meaning your rent or mortgage should not consume more than one-third of your income. In this case, $750 would be a better price range. Granted, some regions will not allow for this, but if you can find an adequate place in the price range, get it. Remember, this is not a permanent situation. Don't get so caught up in image. If you're single, find a roommate, share the bills, and save the money.

Looking at the expenditures on phone, cable, and internet, one would assume that there may be room to compromise. Find a lower cost provider that includes all services. Eliminate those services you don't need. Finally, you may have a new car and not need one. I know they're nice to have, but they are also the most expensive depreciating asset that you will ever purchase. Automobiles are not investments, period. Don't fool yourself into believing otherwise. These are some of the basic principles that a budget makes you address. Let's return to the model.

Liabilities: Accounts Payable		
Description	DR(+)	CR(-)
Electric bill		200.00
Rent		900.00
Gas		30.00
Phone		120.00
Cable		50.00
Car note		533.00
Student loan		.00
Internet		25.68

Total	1858.68

There are no allocations for food or grooming, so we have to make adjustments. Many younger Americans at this point take out loans or take allowance from parents. A note to parents: don't perpetuate this behavior or lack of self discipline by sending money or food. Your children will suffer for the remainder of their lives if you do. Eventually, our system of debt in America will fold, and you don't want to be caught up in the devastation.

At this point, it is best to look at the facts and reduce one or more of your luxuries. You decide which one is lowest on your priority list. Do you have cable just for friends? You may want to trade down your car for a reliable used one. This act could save you $250 on the note and maybe $50 on the insurance. It also may be possible to save $100-250 per month on rent if you find a cheaper place and $450 per month if you find a roommate. That is a total of $400-750 a month and up to $9,000 per year that you saved in a matter of minutes. Using these simple tools to see the bigger picture is helpful. Had we gone willy–nilly, we would have easily overspent and had no food to eat. That's all there is to budgeting. It's not complicated and shouldn't take more than ten minutes a month, once you develop a good system, customized to your needs. I have posted a sample annual budget below that can be filled in with your information. This document is also posted online at www.adamrivon.com so that you may fill it in, print it, and hang it up with your other goals for the year.

Family Budget Year_____				3/20/2006 20:28	
I. Revenues					
	Gross	NET	monthly		
Name:					
Spouse:					
II. Fixed Expenses				*total*	*monthly*
Employer Deductions (401K)	6%			-	-
Deductions (Ins)	2%				
Charity/Tithes	10%				
Additional charity/offerings	1%				
Mortgage	PITI				
Car Note					
III. Variable Expenses				*total*	*monthly*
Household bill/Utilities				-	-
C.C (gas, food, etc)					
AUTO maintenance					
LIST OF GOALS					
ALLOTMENT/SPENDING			0		
			0		

		0		
		0		
		0		
Net savings or Loss				
IV. SAVINGS GOALS		SPENDING		$/month
		THRESHOLD=		
NEW CAR				
PERSONAL				
SCHOOL				
MISC				
INVESTING				
sub total				
TAX Return/Payment				
remainder				

A BUDGET is made of two major sections, which are available cash and planned expenditures. To achieve the next level in your finances, you will need to construct an annual budget. This is the single most important document in your finances. This process will work best if you use a standardized spreadsheet.

NET SAVINGS/LOSS is your gross income minus your planned purchases, taxes, living expenses, charity, etc. The first thing you need to know is how much money you bring home. This is a good time to look at your W-2 form or your last pay stub from the previous year. If you are married, then you will need both spouses' information.

REVENUES

For now, you will use the Social Security wages for a gross amount, because this will include all the extras like auto allowances, etc. You will place the gross amount in section I.

Now, subtract each of the three tax withheld columns (federal, Medicare, and Social Security) and you have your net income from last year. This is your basis.

Next, take from this number all payroll deductions listed on your last pay stub. These include, but aren't limited to, 401K, healthcare, life insurance, etc. Document this information in section II: **fixed expenses/ deductions**. Section II will also include your mortgage payment, existing car notes, and other long-term or fixed debt.

The third section will be labeled variable expenditures/expected purchases and events. There will always be things in life that you desire, but you will need to prioritize them in the beginning of each year. Hopefully, your debt payments aren't consuming all of your remaining cash. At this point, you are going to ask yourself and family what are the major plans and purchases that we expect to make this year. Make a list, placing the most important needs or wants first, and get estimated costs. It is possible that the costs exceed your available cash. This is why you budget. You have to determine what is most important for your life this year.

Section four of your budget will be titled savings and investing goals.

Information in this section will include savings for end-of-the-year purchases and purchases for the upcoming year. For instance, you decide that you would like to purchase a new car in the next one to two years and would like to put as much down as possible, which I recommend, so you decide that you would like to save $200 per month for two years in order to put $5,000 down. You will also include savings for your safety net and allotments for your investments, whether business or pleasure, in this section.

			3/20/2006		
Family Budget Year_____			20:35		

Revenues

	Gross	NET	monthly		
Adam	30000	25500	2125		
Misty	30000	25500	2125		
	60000	51000	4250		

Fixed Expenses				total	**mont hly**
Employer					
Deductions (401K)	6%	-3600	-300	-25824	-2152
Deductions (Ins)	2%	1020	85		
Charity/Tithes	10%	-6000	-500		
Additional					
charity/offerings	1%	-1920	-160		
		-			
Mortgage	PITI	11856	-988		
Car Note		-3468	-289		

Variable Expenses			total	**mont hly**
Household				
bill/Utilities	-5000	-417	-20830	-1736
C.C (gas, food, etc)	-2400	-200		
AUTO maintenance	-1500	-125		

LIST OF GOALS

ALLOTMENT/SPEN

DING	-5200	-433	
JAN *New Chair*	-200	-25	
FEB *Counter-tops*	-1500	-125	next year
JUN *Crown Moldings*	-350	-29	
AUG *TV*	-950	-79	

MAR	computer	-1200	-100		
OCT	Patio Arbor	-480	-40		
MAY	Vacation	-1500	-125		
SEP	New Mattress	-450	-38		
				-46654	-3888
	Net gain or Loss	4246	362		

		SPENDING		/mont
SAVINGS GOALS		*THRESHOLD*=	**-994**	h
CAR	5000			
PERSONAL	2000			
SCHOOL	850			
MISC	0			
INVESTING	1000			
Sub total	(4504)			
TAX RETURN	3000			
remainder	(1504)			

Work-Out Analysis

After you've determined all your wants and savings goals, you have to complete a work-out analysis. This is where you balance the budget.

Side note: here is where our government has the most trouble, because instead of reduction thinking, they at times prefer to print more money. This, in turn, deflates the value of the dollar bills in your pocket and your purchasing power. Other times, they issue treasury or municipal bonds on the assumption that they will have more available cash/tax basis in the future.

You don't have these luxuries, so I recommend that you balance your budget every year! There are three steps in the work-out analysis process.

STEP 1: Attach estimates to your wish list and chart the account or available cash balance. Now, you will most likely need to practice deferred gratification or patience in understanding that you don't have to have it all, right now. Ensure that your total purchases are less than your total available cash. If they're not, you'll need to either cancel them or extend your time horizon into the subsequent years. You will also want to include an allowance for your savings and weekly miscellaneous spending. How you spend your money is totally up to you, but you should always have a plan of attack. If you decided to spend all your money on slot machines, you may have a problem, but at least you've identified it and have given yourself the motivation to either quit or reduce your allotted spending, so that you may have food and shelter.

STEP 2: Develop your time horizon for purchases. You've planned several purchases and activities for the year and have ascertained that you will have the available income/capital, but you won't be able to purchase them all at once. So, take the total price for all your purchases and divide this number by twelve (months in a year). This will give you a basis from which to allocate purchases each month (spending threshold). Take your list, and if the estimated amount of an individual purchase is above the allocated monthly amount or average, then you will have to push it to the following month. This will give you the time to save and ability to purchase the item with cash. Use this technique for all subsequent purchases. Following this guidance will bring you discipline and prosperity. Your debts will diminish and your financial security will increase.

STEP 3: Your final task will be to develop your monthly budget. You've done all the major work and at this point, all you need is to divide all of your annual allotments by the number twelve. Place the purchases in the appropriate and planned months, and all that remains is your very important savings goals. Once you complete this process, your foundation is secure. You now have a platform from which you will make all your future financial decisions.

Due to your hard work and organization, you have just simplified all your financial decisions, and have developed the framework to complete your monthly budget quickly. By including all major purchases, maintenance, and upkeep, you are less likely to be taken by surprise in matters concerning your money.

Here is an example of the budgeting/cash flow system that I use in my household. All payroll formulas are previously calculated in order to simplify computations. All data comes from the previous months bills; loan payments remain constant, and the credit card in this case is paid off every month. In this particular month, there are no planned purchases, this month. The lower section is a rolling review of net worth, and it gives you a panoramic picture of your current position. Finally, the notes sections will describe asterisk areas and any other potential concerns for the month.

DTG	DESCRIPTION	BUDGET	ACTUAL	DTG	DESCRIPTION	BUDGET	ACTUAL
	SPOUSE	$2,500.00			SPOUSE	$2,500.00	
	SPOUSE	$3,200.00			SPOUSE	$3,200.00	
	TAX	(969.00)			TAX	(969.00)	
	DEDUCTIONS	(399.00)			DEDUCTIONS	(399.00)	
1	CHARITY	(570.00)		15	CHARITY	(570.00)	
1	MORTGAGE	(1500.00)		15	LIFE INS	(67.00)	
2	CELL PHONE	(63.00)		15	CAR INS	(50.00)	
4	GAS	(50.00)		15	AUTO LOAN	(288.00)	
		-		18	PEST	-	
8	ELECTRIC	(70.00)					
10	SATELLITE	(88.00)		25	WATER/SEWER	(50.00)	
	EXTRAS*	-		26	INTERNET	(78.00)	
	Yard Care	(100.00)		28	STUDENT LOAN	(145.00)	
					C.C.**	(1500.00)	
	SUB-TOTAL	$1,891.00			SUB-TOTAL	$1,584.00	
	NET SAVINGS OR LOSS					$3,475.00	

	DEBT	EQUITY	SAVINGS/INVESTING	
My Home	(159000.00)	41000	Savings	10000.00
Student Loans	(32000.00)	0	Bank accout #2	2500.00
Car Loan #1	(16554.00)	446	IRA'S	6000.00
Car Loan #2	(8500.00)	-900	401K	12000.00
Credit Cards	(6570.00)	0	401K (2)	6500.00
		40546		37000.00
net worth				77546.00

*=Planned Purchases for the month

**=Food (150), Gas (800), Entertainment (200), Personal care (130), Job expense (vary)

If you are steadfast and are willing to follow these precepts, this is the one task that can propel you to becoming a thousandaire most quickly, because even if you were able to reduce your debt to 10 percent without completing an annual and monthly budget, you would most likely return to your old habits, because there'd be nothing visually or physically causing you to sustain.

When you complete the budget process, you're less likely to accept a department store card, purchase an item on credit that you don't have cash to pay for today, or accept mediocrity in your finances. This will take discipline. The budget is by far your most significant financial document. If you decide to do nothing else that I suggest in this book, complete an annual budget every year and many of the other things will eventually fall into place. Why? A budget bestows upon you knowledge, power, and understanding that you need for your financial well-being. You will receive the knowledge of the facts about your financial picture, the power to change or improve your situation with a pen, and the understanding which comes with this experience and allows you to make the right decisions for your family.

Congratulations on completing this milestone. You can expect to improve your credit, which will increase the number of solicitations sent to you for credit cards and other trinkets that will suck money out of your pockets. Take your name off the solicitation roster and only accept what you have already decided that you need. Be careful in all your endeavors and be wise in all your undertakings.

The annual budget makes you answer the question of what's most important to your family, this year.

Note: Budgeting has never been so simple with the advent of the computer. Consider paying bills online. It allows you to see everything in a snapshot view.

These are commonsense approaches that can be used for the rest of your life. I would like you to take a break now to consider your personal finances, especially if you're married, because more and more Americans cite money as the main reason for divorce, and I don't want you to be part of that negative statistic. Take the time today to make a simple budget for yourself and share the information with your loved ones.

If this was your first budget, you've gained something most never do, and if you've budgeted in the past, this probably put you back on the right track. Learning how to budget is easy, but learning why will make you consistent and wealthy. Many of you may dream of one day being a millionaire, but most will never make a move from middle-class to millionaire status. You can dream to be a millionaire, but becoming a thousandaire is a possibility, and it will give you the proper foundation to sustain and prosper at any level. Conducting an annual budget each year is the first step in conferring thousandaire status.

Real estate values and net worth are excluded from the thousandaire equation in order to equalize the opportunity, because real estate values vary from state to state, and predetermined net worth would exclude individuals who have the right financial structure without currently having the income. The equity built up in your property should be used either to retire or live in. Your equity should only be tapped into for improvements on the home while selling or for continued use, and when applied, should raise the value or capitalize on the current value of the home. You have three options: you can live in the home forever, move up to a bigger home, or move down when finally settling.

I don't at all discount the importance of your net worth, but I would prefer you to have the proper structure. With the proper structure in place, your net worth will automatically rise.

The following are all additional requirements to claim status, and each will be reviewed in depth later: less than 10 percent bad debts, emergency savings, savings, insurance, retirement plans, and estate plans.

You can only claim thousandaire status with all pillars in place. (Disclaimer: I am not an investment representative for any company at the time of these writings, and do no intend to sell you any of the products introduced throughout this book.)

ACTION:

Take the information provided in this chapter and the information that you gathered in the previous chapter and create your personal/family budget today! Visit us online at www.adamrivon.com to download blank copies of these budgeting tools.

"I create an annual budget and use monthly
budgets in order to produce balance and stability
in my decision-making concerning my money!"

Insurance

Retirement/Investing

Savings

Debt Mangement

Monthly Budget

Annual Budget

Balance Books

Three Pillars to Financial Security

| DEBT MANAGEMENT | SAVINGS | INVESTING |

These make up your financial structure. Once you have them, you develop order in your finances. They equate to the past, present, and future. The ways in which you've managed your debt in the past have built good or bad debt ratios. This affords you access to more or less available capital. You need savings here and now to take care of life's sticky situations. If you have enough saved, the pot holes in your life will not become financial abysses. Your investments will take care of you in the future. One day, you will retire, but Social Security and Medicare will not cover all your needs. During the industrial age or in the last generation, you could work for one company your whole life, and for your loyalty, you would receive a pension. We're now in the information age, and companies assume that you are enlightened enough to prepare for your own retirement. If you don't prepare your finances, it will be to your own detriment.

Note: there are still companies out there with pension plans, if you are diligent, consistent, patient and faithful it is still possible to retire with a pension. E.g. the federal government, but the problem with corporate American companies is that if or when pensions become detrimental to the bottom line they can be phased out while and before you are fully vested.

DEBT MANAGEMENT

10 PERCENT BAD DEBT

So, what makes debt good or bad? Let's start with when you make purchases: do you buy appreciating or depreciating assets, assets that make money for you or suck money away? When you procure them, do you make the purchases with cash or credit? Why? Is the credit a card or payment agreement? These are some of the questions to consider.

Here are some terms you should become familiar with:

Assets are anything of material value or usefulness.

Appreciating assets are assets that rise in value with time.

Depreciating assets are assets that decrease in value with time.

The next page will show some examples; associate the terms with the definitions.

1.HOUSE		ASSETS
2.CAR		
3.ARTWORK		
4.ANTIQUES		(d)DEPRECIABLE
5.PURSE		
6.CLOTHES		
7.STOCKS/BONDS		
8.C.D. (certificates of deposit)		(a)APPRECIABLE
9. FURNITURE		
10.ENTERTAINMENT SYSTEM		

Answers: appreciable (1, 3, 7, 8)

It is very important to know the differences between asset types, because when making purchase decisions, you will add to your net worth faster when purchasing appreciating assets. It's the equivalent of taking money out of one pocket and putting it into another--for example, buying a house. You're just moving one asset, money, and putting it in another asset, a new home. You'll take on some associated debt, but in this case, it is considered good for many reasons. First, the government subsidizes the interest payments; in other words, the interest is tax deductible and generally puts you in a position to write off other things that you wouldn't have qualified for through itemized deductions on you tax bill.

Here's a second, maybe less obvious reason. You purchase the house for $150,000 today, and put 10 percent down. Again, you didn't lose $15k, you simply moved it. Assuming an average 5 percent growth per year, you will earn $7,500 in appreciation, without lifting a hand.

By the same token, assume that you live in this home, love and care for it properly over a fifteen-year period. The value of the home will have doubled during this period, and you could potentially sell the home for $300k. You've paid the original mortgage down nearly $45k, and so you gross around $210,000 off the transaction. See the diagram below.

YEAR	TIME	ASSET	LIABILITY	EQUITY
2005	Today	$150,000	$135,000	$15,000
2020	15yrs	$300,000	$90,000	$210,000

A good example of this principle was my first real estate deal in the year 2002. I purchased a rental that was built in 1970. The house was originally purchased for $12,000, and in the year 2002, it was valued at $48,000. I was able to purchase the house at a discount, but you can see that the value had double twice over a thirty-year period. This means that the value appreciated at an average yearly rate of 4.8 percent over the period.

Another reason we exclude real estate and equity in the thousandaire equation is because you should never put all your eggs in one basket. If the value of this home rises and you sell it, you have to buy another one, so the wealth will be held up until you retire and buy down, or pass into eternity. Then the asset can be passed down or used for retirement income.

Now, it's true there are other scenarios, like if you're promoted, have a child, and desire a bigger house that will appreciate in larger numbers and hold your growing family. (These are more advanced scenarios and are outside the scope of our work, now, but know that there are many other valid reasons for upgrading and we will discuss them in later literary works.)

For our uses now, plan on using this money for retirement. The reasons stated above lays out a perfect scenario of good debt. In your lifetime, you should buy as many appreciating assets as possible, and as few depreciating assets as possible.

Here's an example of a depreciating asset: you land a new job, but it's in a place without mass transit, so you need transportation. You purchase a car, but not just any car; you get the one advertisers have had you salivating over for years. You've studied the benefits and imagined yourself gliding down the highway in you brand new____ ___. You decide that you need a car, so you have to have this one, right? You get to the dealership and wouldn't you know it, they have the color and model trim that you desire. The dealer reels you in with some perks, so you make the purchase. They send you to finance and she or he adds on a few trinkets, like an extended warranty. Before you know it, you walk out the door with the keys in your hand. You have a new $30,000 car, with a note at 6 percent interest and higher insurance.

Let's review the purchase.

Start with some basics. Here's a standard rule of thumb about cars: a car can loses 15 to 20 percent of its value each year. A two-year-old car will be worth 80 to 85 percent of its one-year-old value. A three-year-old car will be worth roughly 80 to 85 percent of its two-year-old value. Let's say you have a one-year-old used car worth $12,000 that loses 15 percent of its value each year. At two years old, the car would be worth $10,200. At three years old, it would be worth $8,670.

The depreciation in a car's first year tends to be even steeper. A new-car owner feels the sting immediately. A new car loses a big chunk of its value as soon as you drive it off the lot. Here's why: when purchasing the car, you paid a retail price--the price at which a dealer sells a car. As soon as you're off the lot, the car is worth its wholesale price, the amount a dealer is willing to pay for a car should you turn around and head back. So a brand-spanking-new car or truck loses thousands of dollars of value as soon as you drive it home.

Whatever money you spent on taxes and licensing is gone for good as well. Charlie Vogelheim, editor of Kelley Blue Book, says, "Just the difference between wholesale and retail prices is a large amount of what goes away right away."

Let's look at an example. The base value of a brand-new 2002 Ford Taurus is $19,035, according to the Kelley Blue Book. The wholesale price of a 2002 Ford Taurus with just one hundred miles on it is $15,390, a drop of $3,645 from its transaction price. The wholesale price of a 2002 Ford Taurus with 13,000 miles, roughly a year's worth of driving, is $14,665, nearly 23 percent less than its original transaction price. For more information, see Lucy Lazarony, *Know the deal on auto depreciation*, *26 December2002* <**http://www.bankrate.com/brm/news/auto/20011226a. asp**> (12 May 2005).

What this means to you is that you will have a payment of $479.19 per month. This equates to $28,751.40 paid in five years, and its value will have significantly decreased significantly, while your equity will have increased only slightly. And though you have gained some equity, it will dwindle as time goes by. So, every day you are losing money in interest and depreciation.

YEAR	TIME	ASSET	LIAB	O.E.
2005	Purchase	$19,035	$19,035	-0-
2010	5yrs	$7986	$0	$7986

Recommendation:

Cars are to be purchased for transportation. Purchase a new car only if you are willing to lose 23 percent on your initial purchase price as you drive off the lot. Purchase one- or two-year-old used cars and pay them off quickly. If you have cash, use it, and only purchase vehicles when you need them. If you decide to buy a car for the look and feel of luxury, that's fine too, just understand the full implications of your decision. The intent is not to limit your enjoyment, but to increase your security and peace of mind. Remember, luxury comes with taxes, and the car you drive doesn't have to represent you. Are you a high roller in high debt, or a smart individual who makes sound financial decisions? Men, the ladies may be attracted to you in a particular ride, but they will be much less excited later when they realize that the ride consumes one-third of your income, so you are unable to take them anywhere in it. Rid yourself of the thought process that stigmatizes people based on what they drive. Although auto makers try to personify their creations, you don't have to believe the hype. Your personal value is much greater than anything you will ever drive!

Here again are some examples of good and bad debt:

BAD	GOOD
Car note	Mortgage
Payday loans	Investment Loans (real estate)
Credit cards	Home equity loans (for home improvement only)
Department store cards	Student loans
Furniture loans	

You now understand the differences between good and bad debt. This gives you better understanding of why we set a 10 percent limit on bad debt. Here's how it should work in your budget. Take your net income (after tax) and multiply by 0.10. Whatever the amount, that sets your limit for car notes, new furniture loans, or any other bad debt. If you are already beyond this point, then your next goal is reduction. Stop all purchases, for a season, and focus on lowering your debt. Some people will need to restrict themselves even further, by cutting credit cards. You know yourself and what you can handle.

If you do what is right, by these standards, your situation will improve. I know, from experience, what it is to have nothing at the end of the month for long periods. When I first entered the military as a second lieutenant, I married the lovely lady, Misty, and although we budgeted appropriately for the wedding, Misty was leaving her job in Houston to follow me to North Carolina. She would also be entering graduate school at UNC-Chapel Hill full-time, so I was the bread winner with my Army salary. It was more difficult than I had initially planned. Compounded with all the changes in our life, we had too much month at the end of our money. There probably wasn't a time that we had more than fifty dollars, and this was with no added luxuries. During this period, we didn't have cable TV, we were unable to eat out, go to the movies, go to the clubs, or have any other extracurricular activities. At this point, you've looked at your situation and set some simple short-term goals that will eventually lead you out of your situation. Don't allow others to derail your plans for a night on the town that you may not remember anyway.

STEP ONE: determine whether your situation is permanent or temporary. We knew that Misty's education process was temporary, so she would eventually get a job. We estimated this time to be one and a half years. We also knew that I would soon receive a promotion and increase in pay within the same time frame.

STEP TWO: decide on a course of action. Because our situation was temporary, we were determined to make it out without incurring massive debt, and in fact, we wanted to pay down some of our outstanding loans. Misty had to commute to Chapel Hill from Fayetteville North Carolina in order to save on housing, but we still incurred associated commuter costs. After evaluating the situation further, we realized that we would need to get a student loan in order to pay for all of the costs, and this would also give us relief with some of our other obligations.

STEP THREE: stay the course. With all the changes in our lives and the additional financial challenges, it would was imperative that we stayed in sync. It was very difficult, but we obviously made it. In fact, we came out of the situation and were able to pay off some of the debt that we each inherited with our union, like both of our car notes, and we have actually been without car notes for years.

When you know where you're going and why you are on the track, the race is a lot easier. You have it within yourself to reach your goals. Hold fast to this principle and it will take you a long way on your way to peace and wholeness. Imagine what your life today would be like without a car note. Now, come back to your reality. Just do it!

QUALIFICATIONS FOR THOUSANDAIRE:

1. Produce annual budget
2. Reduce bad debt to under 10 percent

WHY:

This is a critical step that will not only increase your ability to access more capital, but it will give you the flexibility to do more of what you enjoy, instead of allocating the majority of your resources to debt payments. This allows you to spend more time focused on funding your passions, hopes and dreams. What would you being doing today if you had no responsibilities or recurring debt payments? How would your life be different? Would your marriage or personal relationships be affected? These are your motives for change; use them effectively.

Once you have a plan to get your debt under control, you'll be able to adjust your asset allocation. Inside the next few chapters, you will be challenged to rethink how, when, and where you spend your money. For many, this will be a formidable challenge, but if you conquer these tasks, you'll see dramatic life improvements and be well on your way to becoming a thousandaire.

"In order to reduce my bad debts, I will (speak your plan); I can and I will put this plan into action today."

Insurance

Retirement/Investing

Savings

Debt Mangement

Monthly Budget

Annual Budget

Balance Books

SAVINGS

SAFETY NETS

A good seaman will always pack a lifeboat. A parachutist always has a reserve. A leader will always have a back-up plan, and you should always have a financial safety net. What is a safety net, you ask? It is your emergency fund. Life will always happen, and you should always be prepared to react. If you had to jump off a bridge, wouldn't you prefer a bungee cord? In a car accident, wouldn't you have preferred to have an airbag? Why? This is so because it softens the impact. By the same token, in financial pitfalls, wouldn't you prefer to have a buffer? A safety net or emergency fund gets you an airline ticket for the funeral, a rental car when needed, an apartment in a bind, and food during a lay-off. You should never operate in life without needed precautions, and if it means going without for a short time, then so be it. Get your life in order. Living check-to-check is stressful, and more dangerous than driving without a seat belt, or kayaking without a life jacket, and you wonder how bad times tend to drag on--like when your baby is sick and the grandparents are dying. You lose your job and so does your wife. You have a car accident and can't work, but it was an uninsured motorist that hit you. You get sick and don't have enough insurance to cover an operation. I could go on and on, because life happens to the just and unjust. So, you have to be prepared. My recommendation is to put away six months of essential living expenses. We spent time going over your budget and debts, so the calculation is easy. Multiply your basic monthly expenditures by six and you have the needed amount. So, what does this include, mortgage/rent, non-deferrable loans (cars, etc.), utilities, minimal charity? Put away enough money so you can provide for the family's basic needs of food and shelter. During these fragile times when you lose your security (job), it is of ultimate importance psychologically that you have a semblance of order in your household. You may know what it's like to have no income or to be waiting on an unemployment check every week. It isn't easy, and I empathize with those who've passed through these sorts of rough times. I was raised by a single mother and I was the youngest of seven children. Most of my childhood is a blur, but I can recall packing water in the city, drug addicts stealing our electric bill money, and living solely on the two meals provided by my school's system. I do remember attending every elementary school in the city, because we had to move to wherever my mother's job was, but what it taught me was to be prepared, put a little away whenever you can, and always have a fall-back plan.

Now you know what it takes to live one month in your current household, so we use this figure and exclude any and all extras. Know that when things get bad, you'll need to eliminate the fluff. This includes eating out, cable and internet, partying, and any other activity that is not vital to life or producing income. During this time you are surviving. Get in the right mindset. You need to save this money ASAP! Relax, it isn't as difficult as you think, but before you complete any of the other benchmarks to becoming a thousandaire, you must put this pillar in place. How do you begin? We've discussed the budget you have tracking down all of your expenses. Any extra money that you have been using to pay for fruitless items will need to be placed in this pot until your goal is reached. Leaders will take charge of their family finances, and secure this all-important foxhole (critical grounds of security). This is part one of savings. Once your target safety net is attained, then you should put 50 or 60 percent in a C.D. (certificate of deposit). The interest rates are generally higher and penalties for early withdrawal make the money a bit less accessible. Later, you will in fact place 100 percent of the safety net into a C.D., but this is once you have all three pillars in place. Do what it takes, now, because a little discomfort now will go a long way during hard times. Don't procrastinate, because the sooner you complete this goal, the quicker you will move into the more elite status of thousandaire.

SAVINGS-II:

Part two of savings is called deferred gratification. We live in a society today that believes we should have everything that we want and need now, but don't let your potential ruin your reality. It is a fact that the American savings rate is very low. There is also a great debate on the calculation and purpose of this economic statistic. What should be important to you is whether you're saving enough. If you aren't saving, then the answer is simple: no. We've reviewed the need for emergency savings in depth, but just as important is your personal savings for short-term goals and purchases. Marketers study your purchasing habits in order to capitalize on your good and bad habits. It is not their fault that American spending habits are not always healthy. Thousandaires plan their purchases and their lives. Each year, they make a list of all major purchases for that year in an annual budget. Instead of going out and purchasing them all at once or just on a whim, thousandaires make plans to pay cash as often as possible. This allows for more control over your money, and that is what you want. You're able to perform better in emergencies, without stressing over future debt payments. If you lose your job, you can just put a hold on planned purchases for a season. Americans don't always understand or accept this principle. They are accustomed to instant gratification. You speak into a box and pull a meal from a window, you venture around the world and back with the click of a mouse, and so you're not comfortable waiting for anything. Have you ever gotten to the end of a year and said, "I don't know what happened to all my money?" The reason is because you didn't have a plan, and then you had nothing to review or track. After some time, you would probably figure out where some of it went, but may never remember where it all went. Saving allows you to breathe better, because instead of owing money to several companies, you own assets. Use your savings for short-term goals or purchases.

When do you need savings?

- If you want to become a thousandaire
- If you plan to purchase anything with money
- If you intend to vacation or travel during the year

Savings are fundamental. Without them, you will surely succumb to debt. So, how do you do it? There is no sugar coating for this one. You have to be committed to living a better life. If you aren't, then you will never reach this goal. If you are comfortable with the status quo and living check-to-check, then don't follow this advice. Again, don't fall into the mindset that tells you that you need more money to make ends meet. I can show you individuals of all income levels that continue to live check to check. Remember that in goal-setting you aren't required to complete this task today or even this month, but if you truly purpose to change and commit to CANI, constant and never-ending improvement, you will eventually reach this goal.

BENEFITS OF SAVINGS:

- More flexibility with resources
- Improved debt-to-income ratios
- Less buyer's remorse, because you spend more time researching

- Sleeping well at night

QAULIFICATION FOR THOUSANDAIRE:

- Produce annual budget
- Reduce bad debt to less than 10 percent
- Six months emergency savings secured

If you felt peace when you reduced your debt to below 10 percent, you will be euphoric after achieving this landmark in your finances. Your finances are now secure. It will take a tremendous life event to get you off track. You should congratulate yourself with some sort of reward in order to mark this day. Hang out with friends, bake a cake, or take a long hot bath, because you deserve it. In time, you will begin to research and learn better, more efficient ways to continually improve your situation. You are now ready to move into more complicated financials and evoke the principles of multiplication. Up until now, you have been adding and subtracting to reach your goals, but the next chapter will teach you the multiplication tables.

ACTION:

Savings is fundamental, and without at least six month readily available, you will bring undue stress to life's little pitfalls. Take action and open up a savings account today! If the bank is closed, you can open an account over the internet. Decide for yourself what you consider to be a critical dollar amount and that will be your first goal. When I was in college, I determined that $500 would be my minimum safety net. It was enough to get me home if needed, and more than enough to pay any unexpected expenses while away in school. Each case is unique, and you will need to set your first goal according to your situation. Once you meet this goal, you can focus on debt reduction and investing, and then gradually, through systematic deposits, you can attain your thousandaire level.

"I save for the safety of myself, my family, and our lifestyle, because savings is fundamental."

RETIREMENT PLANNING AND INVESTING (10 PERCENT OF INCOME)

The dream for most is to retire rich and retire young, but what are you doing to make it a reality? Many assume that they will always increase their income and so, someday, they'll make up the difference in their spending gap, which is the difference between what a person earns and spends. If the latter is greater, then you are like the government, engaging in deficit spending.

According to the Bureau of Economic Statistics, in 2005 the average American spent $1.04 for every $1.00 made. It's even sadder when you consider the fact that most don't even realize it. So, when and how are they planning to retire? They aren't, because when you fail to plan, you plan to fail. Your final requirement is to develop a plan, or to meet with an advisor to start; no matter what your age, remember it is never too late to start a good thing. Today, many are extending their working lives and even the government has pushed back the official retirement age. So, once you have a safety net goal established, you can begin to invest. This is a life-long process and need not be taken lightly. If you are doing well working a nice job and always improving, then you will someday retire and kick your feet up. When this occurs, you shouldn't have to depend on others for money, but the U.S. Department of Health and Human Services reported that 96 percent of Americans will retire dependant on the government in their December 2005, White House Conference on Aging. I am not one that believes the Social Security will vanish or go bankrupt, because it is, after all, a government program and seniors make up a large percentage of the voting population. Even with this assumption, you still don't want the Social Security Administration to provide for your basic needs of food and shelter. The SSA was developed for the purpose of a societal safety net preventing our country's elderly from falling face-first into poverty. Whether it is right or wrong to garnish wages during your working lifespan, the program has functioned since established, and getting a small stipend for the rest of your retired life is much better than allowing individuals to spend it all pre-retirement and have nothing remaining. The latter would cause the majority to work hard until death or sickness overtakes their bodies.

Retirement planning is essential to happiness and fulfillment, and is also a requirement in becoming a thousandaire. Although you have a great idea that will make you rich, a wise leader will always have a great back-up plan.

Here's what you need to do. Keep it simple. I know you've heard of the Enrons of the world, but the majority of companies today have diversified and independent investment plans, because our lawmakers have made it more difficult to make the same bad mistakes. So, whether your company matches contributions or not, you should still use their services, because many do offer free consultations. If your company will match a portion of your deposits, you should maximize this benefit, period! Let's assume you make $50k per year, and your company will match 50 percent of the first 6 percent of all your contributions. What does this mean? In order to maximize on this offer, you will have to at least contribute 6 percent of your income, or $3,000. The company will then match you dollar-for-dollar at a 50 percent rate, and in this case, it would be $1,500. In other words, the company is going to give you a

3 percent raise, as long as you continue to invest your money. This is in addition to any performance or end-of-year incentives. It's free money that goes into your investment account, but only if you invest first! Some of you are saying that you need that money to live on, and this goes back to deferred gratification. Learn to live on less than you make, because in order to claim thousandaire status, you must invest 10 percent of your gross income. Understand that there are no guaranteed returns, because you're investing in companies that may return profits or losses. A portion of this 10 percent can also be invested in your personal business ventures, but you are required to continue investing at minimum 4 percent in security instruments (mutual funds, stocks, or bonds).

If you're still apprehensive about investing with your company, maybe you should consider another company or job. Just joking! But seriously, outside banks and investment representatives can also assist you. If your company doesn't match your contributions and doesn't offer a similar opportunity, then you should look for a Roth IRA or other investment vehicle. If you're not investing for your futures, what exactly will you do when it gets here and you have no **money**? Regardless of who you use, there are inherent risks associated with investing and you should consider all factors when making this move.

Some things to consider when deciding level of risk are your age, available cash, and comfort with possible money loss.

Businesses boom and bust everyday, and you must understand that you are ultimately investing in a business directly or indirectly. Stocks are a direct investment into a company's capital structure, while mutual funds are a collaboration of several companies' stock. Bonds are debt instruments or means by which companies attain financing for various ventures without diluting or issuing more shares of ownership. The government also issues bonds, but in this case, you're financing a societal project that is under-funded by tax dollars. Know that many times, when taking on this type of investment, the government will give you tax incentives, but not the greatest returns.

The best practice for the majority is going to be a practice called dollar cost averaging. The concept is that you invest a constant percentage of your income over a long period of time, in order to receive the greatest return. The percentage remains constant, so as your pay increases, the dollar amount of your investment also increases. Basing your investment on a percentage is crucial because you can't miss what you never see. In other words, once you begin to live under this principle, it will not feel as though you're penny-pinching. You can still live on the edge, but just to a lower percent. What will occur daily are price fluctuations in the stock market, but because you keep a constant dollar amount, you evoke the buy-low-and-sell-high principle. Trying to speculate when the prices will rise and fall increases risk, and the even the pros have difficulty doing so, but following this principle takes all the guesswork away. Follow the chart below, which documents a twelve-month period of erratic pricing and purchasing verses dollar cost averaging:

Month	Stock Price	Dollar cost shares purchased $500	10 shares per month	30 shares purchased @ expected lows
Jan	48	10.4	$480	
Feb	51	9.8	$510	
Mar	52	9.6	$520	
Apr (low)	50	10	$500	$1500
May	50	10	$500	
June	47	10.6	$470	
July	46	10.8	$460	$1380
Aug (low)	42	11.9	$420	
Sept	48	10.4	$480	
Oct (low)	48	10.4	$480	$1440
Nov	51	9.8	$510	
Dec (low)	53	9.4	$530	$1590
Average value	48.8	123.12 @ $48.8	120 @ $48.80	120 @ $49.25
Amount paid		$6000.00	$5856.00	$5910.00
TODAY'S VALUE	55	$6772.00	$6600.00	$6600.00
PROFIT IF SOLD	1.8	**$772.00**	$744.00	$690.00

Your master key to this principle is continuing to invest in good and bad times. Don't let the market fool you with its schizophrenic performance. Do follow sound financial advice, and if it is time to cut your losses, then do so, but don't stop investing until you reach your predetermined goal, so that you may retire in style. With no financial worries, you will enjoy life more, and you may also live longer. A review of this chart may not impress you, but if you fast forward to your retirement and multiply these amounts by 1,000 ($772,000--$744,000--$690,000), you realize that you could be losing out on tens of thousands.

So, what is your next move? You may need to consult a professional. I will not recommend a particular company, because it is more important that you allow your money to work for you. Stop doing all the work yourself. Be careful to choose an advisor who cares about your financial well-being and isn't just concerned about selling a product. Have a plan or outcome in mind before you speak to an advisor. Here is a good list of interview question to ask when seeking a professional. This list was put out by the Certified Financial Planning board of Standard:

Planner's Name: Company:

Address: Phone:

Date:

1. Do you have experience in providing advice on the topics below? If yes, indicate the number of years: *Retirement planning, Investment planning, Tax planning, Estate planning, Insurance planning, Integrated planning*

2. What are your areas of specialization? What qualifies you in this field?

3. a. How long have you been offering financial planning advice to clients?

   b. How many clients do you currently have?

4. Briefly describe your work history.

5. What are your educational qualifications?

6. What financial planning designation(s) or certification(s) do you hold? CERTIFIED FINANCIAL PLANNER™ or CFP˚, Certified Public Accountant-Personal Financial Specialist (CPA-PFS), Chartered Financial Consultant (ChFC)

7. What licenses do you hold? Insurance, Securities, J.D. CPA

a. Are you personally licensed or registered as an investment adviser representative with a state(s)? If no, why not?

b. Are you or your firm licensed or registered as an investment adviser with the: State(s), Federal Government? If no, why not?

c. Will you provide me with your disclosure document Form ADV Part II or its state equivalent? If no, why not?

10. What services do you offer?

11. Describe your approach to financial planning.

12. a. Who will work with me? Planner, Associate(s)

b. Will the same individual(s) review my financial situation? If no, who will?

13. How are you paid for your services? Fee, Commission, Fee and commission, Salary, Other

14. What do you typically charge?

15. CONFLICT OF INTEREST

a. Do you have a business affiliation with any company whose products or services you are recommending? If yes then please explain:

b. Is any of your compensation based on selling products? If yes please explain:

c. Do professionals and sales agents to whom you may refer me send business, fees or any other benefits to you? If yes please explain:

    d. Do you have an affiliation with a broker/dealer?

    e. Are you an owner of, or connected with, any other company whose services or products I will use?

16. Do you provide a written client engagement agreement? If no, why not

Never enter into any financial relationships with blinders. Take time to evaluate your financial planner just as you would a realtor or any other potential long-term relationship.

BECOMING A THOUSANDAIRE:

- You must invest a minimum of 10 percent of your income in a retirement plan. Exceptions are made for entrepreneurs who are allowed a reduction of 4 percent.
- Take advantage of your employee benefits by maxing out your 401K.
- Don't expect the SSA to take care of you at retirement by planning ahead.

Consult your employer's manual for more information and benefits. Consult a professional or investment representative for more directions and ways to make your money to work for you. These companies include Edward Jones, Meryl Lynch, First Command, Charles Schwab, Fidelity, Ameriprise, etc.

The Jars of Clay

Imagine if you will that you have one million dollars in the bank, all your life savings. Will you ever have to work again? If you are able to make a 6 percent yield on your money, it would be equal to $60k per year. Your annual return may fluctuate, but ask yourself if you could live off this figure. I imagine so, because the average income in America is much lower. So, write the vision and make it plain, set a goal and run, don't walk, towards it. Now, it is a fact that the average American will never even make one million dollars in a lifetime of work, so you're going to need some help. This is why you invest. It will take time before you are able to achieve this goal, but the earlier in life you begin, the better. This is where your wealth starts, and you set your legacy in motion. I also want to point out that retirement shouldn't be your only focus. Set the course and review it every three to six months, and don't take away from this jar, ever. Remember, your goal is to be able to set aside 10 percent of your income for retirement planning.

There are also investments for immediate return. These are separate jars from your retirement, and you should decide before ever spending a dime what you have available to invest. These should only be entered into after or with the advice of professional counsel and intense study and research. They include, but aren't limited to, real estate, franchises, small business ventures, and network marketing. Many of you may be ready to invest today, because you may have attained the previous levels, so I'll go further.

STEP ONE is to figure out what you enjoy doing and learn to make it profitable. If you enjoy skating, maybe you could develop a special skating ring; if you like to bake, try to selling goods part-time for special occasions, community events, etc. Once you know what you want to do, then you will need to write the vision and make it plain.

In **STEP TWO** you will need money, so developing a budget will tell you approximately what is needed to open the doors. Afterwards, you need to determine various methods of financing, and put together a plan of execution.

STEP THREE is project profits. Most people would rather just enjoy having the business, but you need to feed your family and so it is vital for you to plan to make money. How much money will you need to pay for your salary and that of potential workers? You will want to include this in your start-up cost for the first year. What is your bottom line or break-even point? This is your cost of doing business and paying salaries. If you can't make enough money to do both, then your business will fail. There are a host of other considerations in starting a business, but for financial purposes, never enter into a business without conducting your due diligence. That is to take the appropriate care in planning and execution of your new business and consideration of the industry's risk.

Note: unless you are currently in the industry and have made several connections, you are likely to underestimate the cost of doing business. Planning is one of the primary reasons most businesses fail in the first five years.

Once you have the money or financing, you must enter the business with vigor, deliberateness, and methodical execution. Emotions in most cases make a horrible basis for decisions, so try hard to eliminate them.

After your business is off the ground, remember your budget, because unlike a corporation funded by millions of people, your company is probably only funded by you. You won't have the latitude to be indecisive, lackadaisical, or flippant with your money. Finally, most brick and mortar institutions or small businesses fail within the first few years of operation, because they are undercapitalized and poorly planned. Don't let the stats scare you, but be frugal and become an expert in the field. You should run mock trials if possible, before you spend a dime. An investment in yourself is the best investment of all, and once you are ready to rock-n-roll, advertise, promote, and network. I wish you Godspeed on all your future ventures.

Here's a recap:

DEBT MANAGEMENT	SAVINGS	INVESTING

These are the three pillars that make up a financially stable structure. Thousandaires maintain low debt-to-income ratios in order to have more flexibility when making financial decisions. They plan and save for small and large purchases alike, and plan accordingly to pay cash whenever possible. Finally, they plan for retirement, and are rigid investors and wealth builders. So, where do you stand today? Get on track with becoming a thousandaire. I dare you!

THOUSANDAIRE QUALIFICATIONS:

- ¬ Annual Budget
- ¬ 10 percent cap on bad debt
- ¬ Emergency safety net in place
- ¬ 10 percent minimum investments for retirement

Pay close attention to the Jumbo-tron and you will realize the large disparity between your gross and net income. Becoming a thousandaire will force you to live well and below your means. You may be thinking that you're barely living at or above your current income level. How then will you accomplish this feat? You will accomplish it inch by inch, little by little, one day at a time.

Again, never leave the site of a goal without taking a step towards its attainment.

Finally, in the next chapter, we'll discuss how important it is to ensure your family is taken care of after you pass away. You're not trying to make them millionaires, but you also don't want to give them additional debt while paying for your burial. Funerals are expensive and you should be courteous to plan out your affairs.

WHY:

During this generation, we have moved from the industrial age, where our families' members would work for one company their entire lives, and that company was expected to take care of them in retirement. Today, you are on your own! Besides that, you've been paying everyone but yourself since you began working. The government receives 15-33 percent, and your creditors and charities have their hands out, so it is about time that you pay yourself.

"I have to plan for my retirement, because SSI isn't enough! So, I will set aside 10 percent of my gross income and pay myself first."

Protect Yourself, Protect the Family

Congratulations are in order, because if you're reading this section, you know that there's something important in life that needs protection. A drive to success will always lead you back to your family; without them, life is all for not. Money alone doesn't provide happiness.

It is of ultimate importance for you to protect the wealth that you accumulate as a thousandaire. So, I've created three basic levels to make it easier to move forward.

LEVEL I: I believe that every family, once they have devised a plan, should purchase at minimum a death benefit. These are set up to pay for burial expenses. This protects your family from getting into even more debt if you were to pass. This level also includes basic coverage of home and auto. If you do nothing else, consult an agent for this reason.

LEVEL II: This includes Level I and life insurance to cover one year's salary, partially owned assets, and outstanding debt, i.e. your house, car, and student loans. You will want to provide for one year's income so that those you leave will have time to adjust to life without you. These things will make life so much easier to cope with after you leave. It is better to slightly over-insure than to err and not provide enough for your loved ones.

LEVEL III: This is the complete and weatherproof covering for your financial structure. This is your qualification level, and at this level, thousandaires cover the basic insurance needs of Levels I and II, and they take video/digital inventory of all their assets and household items. They have purchased a fire safe for their most important documents. If they currently rent, they have adequate coverage for all their personal property with renter's insurance. They also have bonded or insured their business to protect assets from litigation due to unforeseen events.

Finally, thousandaires have planned for their estates, regardless of the estates' size. In doing so, they have created a final will and testament. If you're worried about this final step and its associated costs, you shouldn't be. You can find and fill out simple and complicated wills online for under $20. Just search for will and testaments. You could also purchase Quicken Will Maker software, which is probably all the detail you may ever need for the least price.

Follow up with an insurance broker or company to discuss your options. I recommend that you find a broker who can provide all your insurance services under one umbrella. This will provide you with economies of a scale in pricing discounts and easy access.

Take away:

You will need adequate protection for your lifestyle and to be prepared for the loss of life. It is also important that you're covered in other areas as well. Thousandaires always ensure that their lives and wealth are protected. This is of ultimate importance to both them and their families.

THOUSANDAIRE QUALIFICATIONS:

1. Annual Budget
2. 10 percent cap on bad debt
3. Emergency safety net in place

4. 10 percent minimum investments for retirement
5. Level III insurance coverage
6. Will and Testament

WHY:

A good man leaves an inheritance
for his children's children.

Proverbs 13:22 NIV bible

ACTION:

Make a plan and work your plan to get a life insurance policy from a reputable company, and if you're riding dirty, stop it, because you're messing with your life, and breaking the law!

By putting it all together you develop a financially secure home.

In the next chapter, we will discuss your credit. We'll talk about your score and how to improve it, what it means, and how it fits in your new paradigm.

*"I am committed to my wealth development; I plan
and make good decisions because I am wealthy!
I insure my family and assets are adequately
insured, because my family is important."*

Insurance

Retirement/Investing

Savings

Debt Mangement

Monthly Budget

Annual Budget

Balance Books

Credit

In God We Trust; All Others Pay Cash.

Anonymous

To many it is a dirty word, but it is one of the most important words in your financial life and times. Your credit history is the basis for evaluation of your ability and willingness to pay for the debts you've incurred. The credit rating scale is 300-850; the average score is 677, and three major agencies receive or compile information from companies that you do business with (TRANSUNION, EQUIFAX, and EXPERION). Each has its own evaluation method, and they are all slightly different. Your part is to make sure that the information each company has is correct. Law mandates that each agency must provide you with a free copy of your report once per year and after anyone denies you credit, based on the information an agency provided. So, when was the last time you evaluated your information? Did you even know that it was free?

Here are the contacts to receive your report:

TRANSUNION

Post Office Box 2000

Chester, PA 19022 www.transunion.com, 800-888-4213

EQUIFAX Information Services LLC

P.O. Box 740241 Atlanta, GA 30374 www.equifax.com, 800-685-1111

EXPERIAN

475 Anton Blvd.

Costa Mesa, CA 92626www.experian.com, 888-397-3742

You can also go to the official site for free annual credit reports, which is sponsored by a collaboration of the three listed agencies: www.annualcreditreport.com; their toll-free number is (877) FACT ACT or 877-322-8228.

They will generally allow you to view the reports online or send you a report in a reasonable time period. What should you do once you receive it?

1. Review the report line by line, and if any of the information is incorrect, you have the right to dispute. Case in point, not long ago, I looked at my report and saw that a credit card that I closed was still on my report. I closed the account because I never used the card and one day several charges appeared. After investigation, the bank realized they had made a mistake and transposed some account numbers. The matter was quickly corrected, but occurred again within a matter of months. This time, correction did not take place as smoothly, and in fact, dragged on for an additional month or so, causing a late payment to be reported for something that I didn't purchase. The bank assured me that it wouldn't be reported, but when I received my report, there it was. So, I quickly disputed the occurrence, citing specific dates and times. The claim was originally denied, but after several faxes, the error was corrected.

2. I recommend that you use the online dispute process if there is an error in reporting. Each agency's website includes this function. The reference company can accept or deny your dispute, and if they deny it, you will have to contact their credit department yourself to explain your position. All requests must be in writing, and you can generally use fax or regular snail mail. This process can sometimes take months, so you will need to be diligent and patient, because most companies don't spend a lot of money on development of efficient credit departments. This causes slower response and execution. Also, be sure to send dispute letters to each of the credit agencies, because they don't communicate with each other. This is why you must view all three reports, because many times one or more of the agencies will not have all or some of your information correct. In the case of fraud, you should call 1-888-567-8688 for an alert. This will require creditors to double verify all transactions that will be added to your report for a given period.

3. Take the initiative to pay off debts that are on the report; don't move money from one card to the next. If you believe you are going to fall behind soon, call whatever company you are indebted to and set up a payment plan or deferral. Tell them you are serious about paying the money you owe in an effort to improve your credit worthiness. Use your budget to figure out what amount of cash you have available to work with and execute this option as planned. Over time, you will see dramatic increases in your score, because open and paid as agreed will increase your score, but if the company writes you off as a bad debt, your score will be dramatically affected.

4. Use your credit for good debt, and use cash for bad debt. Remember, good debt appreciates or puts money in your pocket, and bad debt depreciates and takes money out of your pocketbook.

Many people I've consulted with confess to having bad credit, but can't explain exactly why. The credit report will lay it out for you. It shows the negative and positive factors affecting your score, although the process of computing your score is a guarded secret, which also leads to misconceptions. Here are some of the factors that could affect your score from the:

Payment history: A record of late payments on your current and past credit accounts will lower your score.

Amount owed: Owing too much will lower your score, especially if you're approaching your total credit limit.

Length of credit history: In general, a longer credit history is better.

New accounts: Opening multiple new accounts in a short period of time may lower your score.

Accounts in use: The presence of too many open accounts can lower your score, whether you're using the accounts or not.

Inquiries: Whenever someone else gets your credit report--a lender, landlord, or insurer, for example--an inquiry is recorded on your credit report. A large number of recent inquiries may lower your score.

Public records: Matters of public record such as evictions, bankruptcies, judgments, and collection items may lower your score.

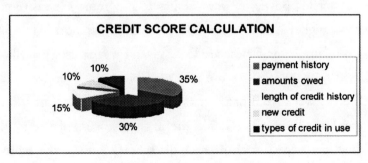

CREDIT SCORE CALCULATION

10% 10% 35% 15% 30%

- payment history
- amounts owed
- length of credit history
- new credit
- types of credit in use

Don't just accept what people tell you; know the facts for yourself. The information is free, but will not include your actual FICO score. You will have to pay for your FICO score, unless you sign up for credit monitoring. I don't recommend you take this service, unless you really need the security. This service can help if you have been a victim of fraud and suspect that you are still susceptible; otherwise, you are better off saving the small monthly fee and keeping up with your records on a quarterly basis.

Here's how: you have the liberty of receiving a free credit report each year from each of the three major reporting agencies, but no one says that you must retrieve them all at the same time. Take one for yourself and spouse every four months. Review the data for each report line by line, and generally, you will not have much that has changed after your initial correction of the report. If all is well, then no action is needed, and you saved money for the monitoring, and saved yourself from embarrassment by preventing yourself from being denied in the future.

Okay, so you do all that you can to ensure your information is correct, but what is the big deal about credit? Credit is your financial life's blood. If your scores are high and your income is stable, you can get lower interest rates and higher loan amounts, because companies assess you as a low risk for repayment. With lower interest rates, you increase your purchasing power, or your ability to buy more expensive goods. Banks like higher scores, so they allow you to access more loan vehicles, like non-secure loans. These are loans given for whatever you like, and are based on your credit score and available cash. I receive calls and emails every week from bankers asking if I need some more money to do something. Remember, banks are in the business of making loans and they love people with high credit scores, because the score tells them who can be trusted to pay back debts with interest. You may also know of many job opportunities, which are predicated on your credit.

Finally, a higher credit score will give you joy, marking your success level in managing your personal finances.

Here are some tips to improve your score:

v   Start by learning what your score is today. Order your free report!

v   Correct any information on your report by following the dispute process on all reports.

v   To lower your overall balances, focus on paying more towards the card with the highest interest rate!

v   Don't except any new credit cards or open any new lines of credit.

v   Pay all credit accounts on time.

Remember, your score is a reflection of your past seven-year history and cannot be fixed in one day. Before you request the services of a repair company, take these simple steps. You'll better understand your unique situation by reviewing it as a creditor. Would you extend credit to another person with a similar credit history, or would you be apprehensive? Historically, credit was extended based on people's word, and believe it or not, it still is. Today, credit scores allow lenders across the nation to make decisions in an instant, but without the biases of race, color, religion, or gender. Be true to yourself and your creditors, by keeping your word and paying your debts.

DOS AND DON'TS

*   Don't co-sign for anyone that you don't have authority over.
*   Don't use multiple credit cards as a source of income or cash unless you are able to pay the cards off each month.

- Do pay all debts on time and if there is a problem, call your lender.
- Do look for ways to improve your credit score legally at <u>www.myfico.com</u> under the credit information tab.

THOUSANDAIRE QUALIFICATIONS:

1. Annual Budget
2. 10 percent cap on bad debt
3. Emergency safety net in place
4. 10 percent minimum investments for retirement
5. Level III insurance coverage
6. Will and Testament
7. 700 average credit score

By following the thousandaire system, you will always live your life in abundance, and be able to take care of yourself without the assistance of others. Start today living and enjoying everyday life.

I pray that you remain steadfast in your convictions to live better on the inside, and the day shall come when it shows on the outside. Now is the time to pick up the goals that you wrote earlier, and review and fine tune them.

Here is your final challenge: the next time you consider developing a serious or intimate relationship with someone, find out first if they are a thousandaire or are moving toward this effort. It is a known fact that mismanaged finances and trust are the leading causes for divorce. By asking this simple question, you can know a potential spouse's status without coming off as being overly concerned with income.

If you're already married, please allow your spouse to read this book before you berate him or her with new ideas. You all have to be on one accord in order to complete the required steps. Also, consider combined accounts for more efficiency while budgeting. For more information or lessons learned, you can visit me on the web.

I would like to congratulate those of you who have already met the thousandaire challenge. Visit me online, confer your status, and share your success to encourage others. For all others, you now have the knowledge necessary to balance your checkbooks and budgets, keep more money, live better, and stay out of debt. Meeting this challenge will set the course for your personal financial legacy, and by doing so, you will be able to bless your children's children.

www.adamrivon.com

Resource Guide

The following is a list of recommended books and audio that will enhance the seven steps we've reviewed and assist you in a total life transformation.

RECOMMENDED READING

*The 7 Habits of Highly Effective People by Stephen R. Covey. New York, NY: Simon & Schuster, 1989.

*The Millionaire Next Door by Thomas J. Stanley and William D. Danko. Marietta, GA: Longstreet Press, Inc., 1996.

*The Power of Focus by Jack Canfield an

d Mark Victor Hansen. Deerfield Beach, FL: Health communications, Inc., 2000.

*Rich Dad, Poor Dad by Robert Kiyosaki. New York, NY: Warner Books, 1999.

*The Richest Man in Babylon by George S. Clason. New York, NY: Penguin Books, 1989.

*Think & Grow Rich by Napoleon Hill. New York, NY: Fawcett Crest Books/ CBS Inc., Division of Ballantine Books, 1960.

*Thinking for a Change by John C. Maxwell. Warner Books, 2003.

AUTOBIOGRAPHY/BIOGRAPHY

*Made in America by Sam Walton. New York, NY: Bantam Books, 1993.

AUDIO

"Get the Edge" by Anthony Robbins. Live Recording. San Diego, 2001.

Printed in the United States
77318LV00007B/47